MW01626225

Falconer's Log Book
1st Edition
8.5 x 11 inch, 12-month format
(Out of Print)
1,350 copies printed between February 1994 and December 2005

Falconer's Log Book
2nd Revised Edition
7 x 8.5 inch, 8-month format
400 copies printed between January 2006—October 2008

Falconer's Log Book
3rd Edition
7 x 8.5 inch, 12-month format
Print-On-Demand Version

BETTER HAWKING BOOKS
EAGLEWING PUBLISHING
Post Office Box 188
Warrens, Wisconsin 54666

Catalog available on-line at:

www.EagleWingPublishing.Com

The Falconer's Logbook is also available as a computer program.
All you do is enter the raw data each day.
The software draws both of the charts for you!
See the website catalog for details.

Printed in the United States of America
ISBN 1-885054-24-6

Log Book for

____

____
Band Number

____
Species

____
Gender

Trapped at ______________________________ **Date** ____________________

Or

Acquired from ____________________________ **Date** ____________________

Lineage: **Falcon / Female** ____________________ **Band Number** ____________

Tiercel / Male _____________________ **Band Number** ____________

Notes:

____
____
____
____
____
____
____
____
____
____
____

How to Use the Daily Log Sheet

For each day of the month, record the following information:

1. Record the hawk or falcon's Starting Weight either in grams or ounces. This is the weight at the beginning of your training or hunting session.
2. Record the overnight Low Temperature.
3. Record the current High Temperature. This is the temperature outside while you were training or hunting.
4. Record the Food Type you fed to your hawk or falcon. Examples are Chick, Quail, Mice, Rabbit. Not all food is the same. A few ounces of pigeon breast is probably as nutritious and fat producing as are twice as many ounces of day-old chicks. Therefore, during a cold night, your hawk will maintain her weight better with pigeon than with chicks. You need to track and grow to understand this relationship!
5. Record the Ending Weight after feeding.
6. Record the hawk or falcon's performance Rating. 1=Poor or Lost, 2=Fair, 3=Good, 4=Very Good, 5=Excellent or a Kill.
7. Enter the number of head of game caught.
8. Record the type of game caught.
9. Write down other thoughts, experiences, and comments.

How to Use the Charts

1. On the Charted Weight Per Date chart, found facing each log sheet, first fill in the probably weight range your hawk or falcon will be in for the month. You will have to estimate this but it is important to do so at the start of each recording period. Enter this range in the Weight column. This weight can be in ounces or grams. Make the incremental divisions in equal jumps; each quarter ounce or 10 grams, for example. **Always put the low end of the range at the bottom of the chart and number upwards**.

2. Each day, after filling in the log sheet, place a mark in the proper cell of the chart which corresponds to that day's weight. Draw a line between this mark and the mark from the previous day to begin to draw the trend line.

3. Also, each day, after filling in the log sheet, place a mark in the proper cell of the Charted Rating Per Date chart. Remember that the number 5 means an excellent falconry day, perhaps even a day when your hawk or falcon caught wild game. Otherwise, if she flew like a highly trained, skilled, conditioned, and cooperative hunting partner, give her a 5! The goal of all of this record-keeping and charting is to string together as many 5 days as you can. Again, draw a line from the previous day's mark to show the trend line.

4. Monitor the two trend lines in accordance with the information provided in the Interpreting the Chart Trend Lines section of this log book. Eventually, you will notice when your hawk or falcon was a '5' and what her weight was on that date. You will also begin to see other important trends as you use the charts. Trends which will help you keep from losing your hawk and from starving her. Remember, it is important that every falconer exercise self-discipline and consistency. Keeping a log book is an important discipline to establish and maintain.

Interpreting the Chart Trend Lines

(DISCLAIMER: *The following log sheet entries and accompanying charts are fictitious. They serve only for illustration purposes. Do not use them as a guide for how much or what to feed your hawk or falcon under real-life situations.)*

Through disciplined use of the log book, you will learn the optimum flying weight for your hawk or falcon. You also will understand the relationships between weight and performance, weight and overnight low temperature, weight and amount of food given, weight and the type of food given. You also can learn how temperature, amount of food, and food type effect your hawk or falcon's weight.

Here are some points to consider. A newly trapped bird will generally be too high in weight (too fat) to use effectively in falconry. Her weight must be trimmed somewhat to achieve the desired responsiveness to manning and training. Still more weight may need to be trimmed to be successful in hunting. But how to know when you have trimmed enough? Too much?

1. Look at the sample chart for the first ten days in October. During this period, our fictitious hawk's weight was reduced gradually until on the 7th of the month the log book shows that she had a '5' rating day. This was the day when she flew like a properly trained and conditioned falconry bird. So, the Rating trend line between the 1st and 7th draws gradually upward. This is important to notice. With newly trained birds, birds coming out of the molt, or birds coming off of an extended period of inactivity, the Weight chart should show a gradual downward trend with a corresponding upward Performance Rating trend. From a graphical perspective a descending Weight trend line with an ascending Performance Rating trend line (Descending / Ascending) is a good thing.

2. On the 7th of the month, our fictitious hawk caught a jackrabbit and was gorged on it (fed a full crop). Notice that the Weight trend line begins to redraw from the top of the chart downward until the 11th when her flying weight is achieved again. Also notice that the Rating chart redraws from the bottom to the top again. A descending Weight trend line with an ascending Rating trend line (Descending / Ascending) is good.

3. Now notice what happened on the 12th. The hawk was not responding well so washed meat was fed to her. Unfortunately, a severe cold snap hit that same night. This caused the hawk to lose too much weight. The Weight trend line was still going down, BUT the Performance Rating trend line drew downward also. This is a dangerous situation. Remember, hawks and falcons that are in too low a condition (starving) often times respond exactly in the same way as a bird in too high of a condition (fat), at least at first. So, beware of a descending Weight trend line with a descending Performance Rating trend line. Descending / Descending always means trouble.

4. This fictional episode highlights an important point. Even at the proper weight, a falconer should not reduce his hawk's weight on days when she perhaps rates a '5' but does not catch anything. Why? Because the hawk must be given sufficient opportunities to make a kill. Being at hunting weight does not guarantee that the hawk will be successful on wild game. She must be given plenty of opportunities under favorable circumstances. A good falconer knows this and will not reduce his hawk's weight ***when he was unable to produce enough game for her to chase***.

5. From the above discussion, it is clear that a Descending Weight trend line with an Ascending Performance Rating trend line is good. It is also critical to note that a Descending Weight trend line with a Descending Performance Rating trend line means trouble. It is then obvious that an Ascending Weight trend line most likely will mean a Descending Performance Rating trend line (Ascending / Descending) since the hawk is not getting hungry (sharp) enough to perform well as a falconry bird.

6. The only other combination of relationships between the two trend lines is an Ascending Weight with an Ascending Performance trend lines (Ascending / Ascending). It does happen! This means that the hawk has either gained more muscle, the temperatures during the hunts are cooler, the hawk is tuning into the falconer's routine, or a combination of these factors. In any case, an Ascending / Ascending (or an Ascending Weight trend line with a constant '5' Rating) is to be watched for and enjoyed when it happens. The hawk or falcon will be flying stronger, in a higher condition, while still aggressively chasing game. When this happens, you know that you have successfully established your routine in her life. She is comfortable with her surroundings and with you. Be on the lookout, however, for any changes in weather or the routine that might cause her to revert somewhat to her old ways. For example, if she were flying an ounce heavier during January's frigid cold—and it suddenly warms to 50 degrees—DO NOT FLY HER. What is a good flying weight for freezing weather is a lost hawk weight in warmer weather. Yet, being able to fly your hawk or falcon at weights higher than absolutely necessary is a sign of your becoming a more skilled falconer.

REVIEW:

Descending / Ascending -	**Good;** the normal process for training and hunting.
Descending / Descending -	**BAD;** bird could be starving or ill.
Ascending / Descending -	**Normal;** usually, the fatter a hawk or falcon gets, the poorer her performance becomes, except…
Ascending / Ascending -	**Excellent;** the hawk or falcon is responsive at higher and stronger weights. She is enjoying being with you! Well Done!!

October / 2005 FOR ILLUSTRATION ONLY—FICTIONAL LOG ENTRIES

Date	Starting Weight	Low Temp	High Temp	Food Type	Ending Weight	Rating 1=Poor 5=Great	# Caught	Game Caught
1	36 Ounces	40's	50's	None	36	1		
Comment	Still too fat. Fed on lure yesterday.							
2	35.5	40's	50's	None	35.5	1		
Comment	Almost jumped to the fist but not quite ready.							
3	35.5	40's	50's	Wash Bheart	38	1		
Comment	Flying upwards of 10 feet on creance. Vertical jumps in the garage.							
4	35.25	40's	50's	Wash Bheart	37	2		
Comment	Flew length of creance: 25 feet.							
5	34.75	40's	50's	Quail	36	3		
Comment	Now showing some interest! Just a couple of free flights.							
6	34.00	30's	40's	Wash Bheart	35.5	4		
Comment	Finally! We should be ready to go tomorrow.							
7	33.50	30's	40's	Beefheart	40	5	1	Jackrabbit
Comment	Caught jackrabbit in hard flight. Responded well to fist.							
8	36	30's	40's	None	36	1		
Comment	Rested her today. Still fat and happy from yesterday!							
9	35	30's	40's	Wash Bheart	36	1		
Comment	A few dozen vertical jumps indoors just to keep her active.							
10	34	30's	40's	Chick	35.5	3		
Comment	Flew her around the backyard. She is ready.							
11	33.50	30's	40's	Quail	34.50	4		
Comment	Hunted today. She did not seem very interested in the jackrabbits. Wanted a cottontail!							
12	33.00	20's	30's	Wash Bheart	35	4		
Comment	Flying hard but not willing to crash the cover like she knows how to. Wonder why?							
13	32.25	0's	10's	Quail	38	1		
Comment	TOO LOW! Very cold last night. Weight control got away from me...							
14	36	20's	20's	Jackrabbit	38	1		
Comment	Did not work her today. Letting her recover fully. Weather warming up too.							

Date	Starting Weight	Low Temp	High Temp	Food Type	Ending Weight	Rating 1=Poor 5=Great	# Caught	Game Caught
15	34	20's	20's	Jackrabbit	37	5		
Comment	She is back to her old self and flying a bit heavier with the colder day-time temperatures.							

FOR ILLUSTRATION ONLY—FICTIONAL LOG ENTRIES

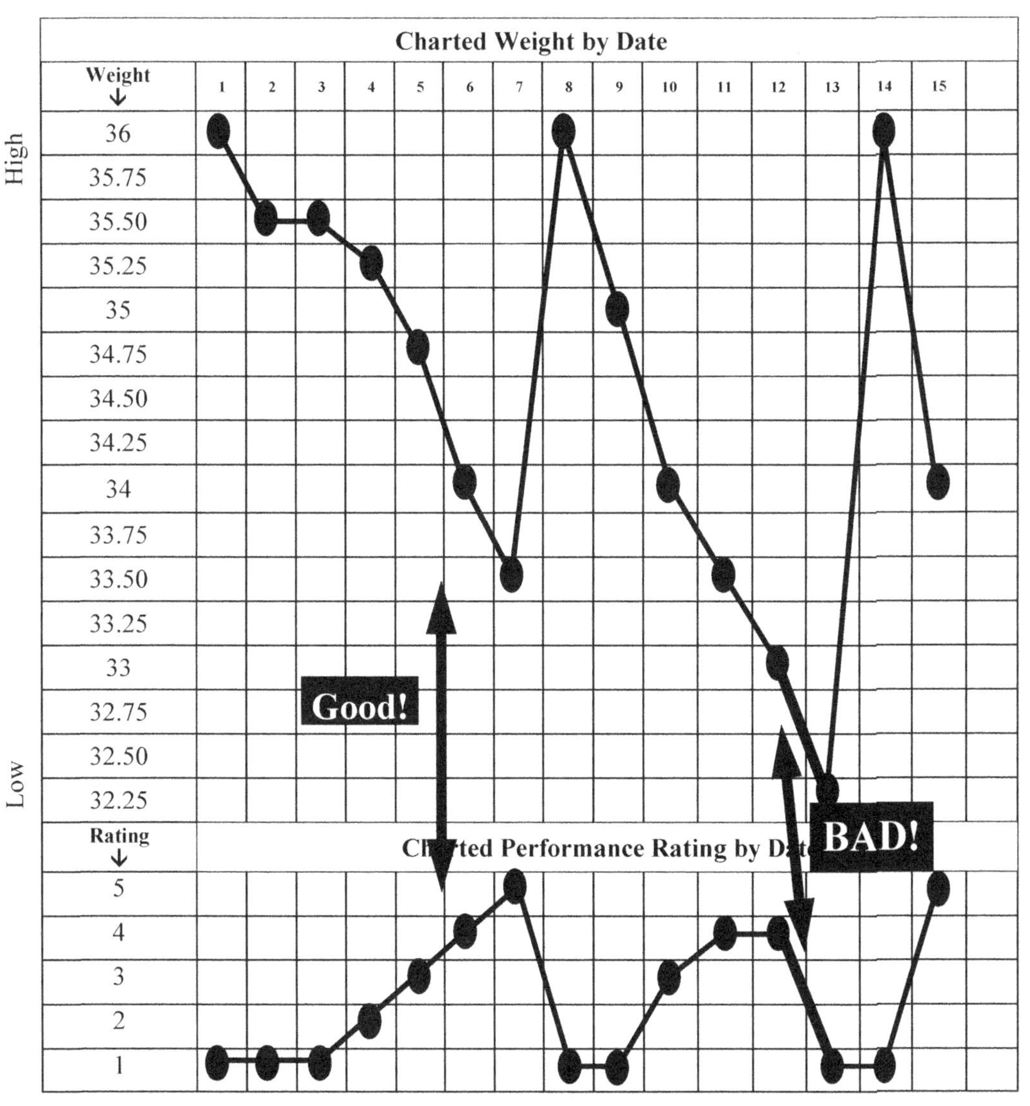

Photo Album

Month / Year:

Date	Starting Weight	Low Temp	High Temp	Food Type	Ending Weight	Rating 1=Poor 5=Great	# Caught	Game Caught
1								
Comment								
2								
Comment								
3								
Comment								
4								
Comment								
5								
Comment								
6								
Comment								
7								
Comment								
8								
Comment								
9								
Comment								
10								
Comment								
11								
Comment								
12								
Comment								
13								
Comment								
14								
Comment								

Date	Starting Weight	Low Temp	High Temp	Food Type	Ending Weight	Rating 1=Poor 5=Great	# Caught	Game Caught
15								
Comment								

Charted Weight by Date																
Weight ↓	1	2	3	4	5	6	7	8	9	10	11	12	13	14	15	
High																
Low																
Rating ↓	Charted Performance Rating by Date															
5																
4																
3																
2																
1																

Month / Year:

Date	Starting Weight	Low Temp	High Temp	Food Type	Ending Weight	Rating 1=Poor 5=Great	# Caught	Game Caught
16								
Comment								
17								
Comment								
18								
Comment								
19								
Comment								
20								
Comment								
21								
Comment								
22								
Comment								
23								
Comment								
24								
Comment								
25								
Comment								
26								
Comment								
27								
Comment								
28								
Comment								
29								
Comment								

Date	Starting Weight	Low Temp	High Temp	Food Type	Ending Weight	Rating 1=Poor 5=Great	# Caught	Game Caught
30								
Comment								
31								
Comment								

Charted Weight by Date																
Weight ↓	16	17	18	19	20	21	22	23	24	25	26	27	28	29	30	31
High																
Low																
Rating ↓	Charted Performance Rating by Date															
5																
4																
3																
2																
1																

Month / Year:

Date	Starting Weight	Low Temp	High Temp	Food Type	Ending Weight	Rating 1=Poor 5=Great	# Caught	Game Caught
1								
Comment								
2								
Comment								
3								
Comment								
4								
Comment								
5								
Comment								
6								
Comment								
7								
Comment								
8								
Comment								
9								
Comment								
10								
Comment								
11								
Comment								
12								
Comment								
13								
Comment								
14								
Comment								

Date	Starting Weight	Low Temp	High Temp	Food Type	Ending Weight	Rating 1=Poor 5=Great	# Caught	Game Caught
15								
Comment								

	Charted Weight by Date															
Weight ↓	1	2	3	4	5	6	7	8	9	10	11	12	13	14	15	
High																
Low																
Rating ↓	Charted Performance Rating by Date															
5																
4																
3																
2																
1																

Month / Year:

Date	Starting Weight	Low Temp	High Temp	Food Type	Ending Weight	Rating 1=Poor 5=Great	# Caught	Game Caught
16								
Comment								
17								
Comment								
18								
Comment								
19								
Comment								
20								
Comment								
21								
Comment								
22								
Comment								
23								
Comment								
24								
Comment								
25								
Comment								
26								
Comment								
27								
Comment								
28								
Comment								
29								
Comment								

Date	Starting Weight	Low Temp	High Temp	Food Type	Ending Weight	Rating 1=Poor 5=Great	# Caught	Game Caught
30								
Comment								
31								
Comment								

Charted Weight by Date																
Weight ↓	16	17	18	19	20	21	22	23	24	25	26	27	28	29	30	31
High																
Low																
Rating ↓	Charted Performance Rating by Date															
5																
4																
3																
2																
1																

Month / Year:

Date	Starting Weight	Low Temp	High Temp	Food Type	Ending Weight	Rating 1=Poor 5=Great	# Caught	Game Caught
1								
Comment								
2								
Comment								
3								
Comment								
4								
Comment								
5								
Comment								
6								
Comment								
7								
Comment								
8								
Comment								
9								
Comment								
10								
Comment								
11								
Comment								
12								
Comment								
13								
Comment								
14								
Comment								

Date	Starting Weight	Low Temp	High Temp	Food Type	Ending Weight	Rating 1=Poor 5=Great	# Caught	Game Caught
15								
Comment								

	Charted Weight by Date																
	Weight ↓	1	2	3	4	5	6	7	8	9	10	11	12	13	14	15	
High																	
Low																	
	Rating ↓	Charted Performance Rating by Date															
	5																
	4																
	3																
	2																
	1																

Month / Year:

Date	Starting Weight	Low Temp	High Temp	Food Type	Ending Weight	Rating 1=Poor 5=Great	# Caught	Game Caught
16								
Comment								
17								
Comment								
18								
Comment								
19								
Comment								
20								
Comment								
21								
Comment								
22								
Comment								
23								
Comment								
24								
Comment								
25								
Comment								
26								
Comment								
27								
Comment								
28								
Comment								
29								
Comment								

Date	Starting Weight	Low Temp	High Temp	Food Type	Ending Weight	Rating 1=Poor 5=Great	# Caught	Game Caught
30								
Comment								
31								
Comment								

	Charted Weight by Date																
	Weight ↓	16	17	18	19	20	21	22	23	24	25	26	27	28	29	30	31
High																	
Low																	
	Rating ↓	Charted Performance Rating by Date															
	5																
	4																
	3																
	2																
	1																

Month / Year:

Date	Starting Weight	Low Temp	High Temp	Food Type	Ending Weight	Rating 1=Poor 5=Great	# Caught	Game Caught
1								
Comment								
2								
Comment								
3								
Comment								
4								
Comment								
5								
Comment								
6								
Comment								
7								
Comment								
8								
Comment								
9								
Comment								
10								
Comment								
11								
Comment								
12								
Comment								
13								
Comment								
14								
Comment								

Date	Starting Weight	Low Temp	High Temp	Food Type	Ending Weight	Rating 1=Poor 5=Great	# Caught	Game Caught
15								
Comment								

Charted Weight by Date																
Weight ↓	1	2	3	4	5	6	7	8	9	10	11	12	13	14	15	
High																
Low																

Rating ↓	Charted Performance Rating by Date															
5																
4																
3																
2																
1																

Month / Year:

Date	Starting Weight	Low Temp	High Temp	Food Type	Ending Weight	Rating 1=Poor 5=Great	# Caught	Game Caught
16								
Comment								
17								
Comment								
18								
Comment								
19								
Comment								
20								
Comment								
21								
Comment								
22								
Comment								
23								
Comment								
24								
Comment								
25								
Comment								
26								
Comment								
27								
Comment								
28								
Comment								
29								
Comment								

Date	Starting Weight	Low Temp	High Temp	Food Type	Ending Weight	Rating 1=Poor 5=Great	# Caught	Game Caught
30								
Comment								
31								
Comment								

Charted Weight by Date																
Weight ↓	16	17	18	19	20	21	22	23	24	25	26	27	28	29	30	31
High																
Low																
Rating ↓	Charted Performance Rating by Date															
5																
4																
3																
2																
1																

Month / Year:

Date	Starting Weight	Low Temp	High Temp	Food Type	Ending Weight	Rating 1=Poor 5=Great	# Caught	Game Caught
1								
Comment								
2								
Comment								
3								
Comment								
4								
Comment								
5								
Comment								
6								
Comment								
7								
Comment								
8								
Comment								
9								
Comment								
10								
Comment								
11								
Comment								
12								
Comment								
13								
Comment								
14								
Comment								

Date	Starting Weight	Low Temp	High Temp	Food Type	Ending Weight	Rating 1=Poor 5=Great	# Caught	Game Caught
15								
Comment								

	Charted Weight by Date															
Weight ↓	1	2	3	4	5	6	7	8	9	10	11	12	13	14	15	
High																
Low																

Rating ↓	Charted Performance Rating by Date															
5																
4																
3																
2																
1																

Month / Year:

Date	Starting Weight	Low Temp	High Temp	Food Type	Ending Weight	Rating 1=Poor 5=Great	# Caught	Game Caught
16								
Comment								
17								
Comment								
18								
Comment								
19								
Comment								
20								
Comment								
21								
Comment								
22								
Comment								
23								
Comment								
24								
Comment								
25								
Comment								
26								
Comment								
27								
Comment								
28								
Comment								
29								
Comment								

Date	Starting Weight	Low Temp	High Temp	Food Type	Ending Weight	Rating 1=Poor 5=Great	# Caught	Game Caught
30								
Comment								
31								
Comment								

Charted Weight by Date																	
	Weight ↓	16	17	18	19	20	21	22	23	24	25	26	27	28	29	30	31
High																	
Low																	
	Rating ↓	Charted Performance Rating by Date															
	5																
	4																
	3																
	2																
	1																

Month / Year:

Date	Starting Weight	Low Temp	High Temp	Food Type	Ending Weight	Rating 1=Poor 5=Great	# Caught	Game Caught
1								
Comment								
2								
Comment								
3								
Comment								
4								
Comment								
5								
Comment								
6								
Comment								
7								
Comment								
8								
Comment								
9								
Comment								
10								
Comment								
11								
Comment								
12								
Comment								
13								
Comment								
14								
Comment								

Date	Starting Weight	Low Temp	High Temp	Food Type	Ending Weight	Rating 1=Poor 5=Great	# Caught	Game Caught
15								
Comment								

	Charted Weight by Date																
	Weight ↓	1	2	3	4	5	6	7	8	9	10	11	12	13	14	15	
High																	
Low																	
	Rating ↓	Charted Performance Rating by Date															
	5																
	4																
	3																
	2																
	1																

Month / Year:

Date	Starting Weight	Low Temp	High Temp	Food Type	Ending Weight	Rating 1=Poor 5=Great	# Caught	Game Caught
16								
Comment								
17								
Comment								
18								
Comment								
19								
Comment								
20								
Comment								
21								
Comment								
22								
Comment								
23								
Comment								
24								
Comment								
25								
Comment								
26								
Comment								
27								
Comment								
28								
Comment								
29								
Comment								

Date	Starting Weight	Low Temp	High Temp	Food Type	Ending Weight	Rating 1=Poor 5=Great	# Caught	Game Caught
30								
Comment								
31								
Comment								

Charted Weight by Date																	
	Weight ↓	16	17	18	19	20	21	22	23	24	25	26	27	28	29	30	31
High																	
Low																	
	Rating ↓	Charted Performance Rating by Date															
	5																
	4																
	3																
	2																
	1																

Month / Year:

Date	Starting Weight	Low Temp	High Temp	Food Type	Ending Weight	Rating 1=Poor 5=Great	# Caught	Game Caught
1								
Comment								
2								
Comment								
3								
Comment								
4								
Comment								
5								
Comment								
6								
Comment								
7								
Comment								
8								
Comment								
9								
Comment								
10								
Comment								
11								
Comment								
12								
Comment								
13								
Comment								
14								
Comment								

Date	Starting Weight	Low Temp	High Temp	Food Type	Ending Weight	Rating 1=Poor 5=Great	# Caught	Game Caught
15								
Comment								

	Charted Weight by Date																
	Weight ↓	1	2	3	4	5	6	7	8	9	10	11	12	13	14	15	
High																	
Low																	
	Rating ↓	Charted Performance Rating by Date															
	5																
	4																
	3																
	2																
	1																

Month / Year:

Date	Starting Weight	Low Temp	High Temp	Food Type	Ending Weight	Rating 1=Poor 5=Great	# Caught	Game Caught
16								
Comment								
17								
Comment								
18								
Comment								
19								
Comment								
20								
Comment								
21								
Comment								
22								
Comment								
23								
Comment								
24								
Comment								
25								
Comment								
26								
Comment								
27								
Comment								
28								
Comment								
29								
Comment								

Date	Starting Weight	Low Temp	High Temp	Food Type	Ending Weight	Rating 1=Poor 5=Great	# Caught	Game Caught
30								
Comment								
31								
Comment								

Charted Weight by Date																
Weight ↓	16	17	18	19	20	21	22	23	24	25	26	27	28	29	30	31
High																
Low																
Rating ↓	Charted Performance Rating by Date															
5																
4																
3																
2																
1																

Month / Year:

Date	Starting Weight	Low Temp	High Temp	Food Type	Ending Weight	Rating 1=Poor 5=Great	# Caught	Game Caught
1								
Comment								
2								
Comment								
3								
Comment								
4								
Comment								
5								
Comment								
6								
Comment								
7								
Comment								
8								
Comment								
9								
Comment								
10								
Comment								
11								
Comment								
12								
Comment								
13								
Comment								
14								
Comment								

Date	Starting Weight	Low Temp	High Temp	Food Type	Ending Weight	Rating 1=Poor 5=Great	# Caught	Game Caught
15								
Comment								

Charted Weight by Date																
Weight ↓	1	2	3	4	5	6	7	8	9	10	11	12	13	14	15	
High																
Low																
Rating ↓	Charted Performance Rating by Date															
5																
4																
3																
2																
1																

Month / Year:

Date	Starting Weight	Low Temp	High Temp	Food Type	Ending Weight	Rating 1=Poor 5=Great	# Caught	Game Caught
16								
Comment								
17								
Comment								
18								
Comment								
19								
Comment								
20								
Comment								
21								
Comment								
22								
Comment								
23								
Comment								
24								
Comment								
25								
Comment								
26								
Comment								
27								
Comment								
28								
Comment								
29								
Comment								

Date	Starting Weight	Low Temp	High Temp	Food Type	Ending Weight	Rating 1=Poor 5=Great	# Caught	Game Caught
30								
Comment								
31								
Comment								

Charted Weight by Date																
Weight ↓	16	17	18	19	20	21	22	23	24	25	26	27	28	29	30	31
High																
Low																

Rating ↓	Charted Performance Rating by Date															
5																
4																
3																
2																
1																

Month / Year:

Date	Starting Weight	Low Temp	High Temp	Food Type	Ending Weight	Rating 1=Poor 5=Great	# Caught	Game Caught
1								
Comment								
2								
Comment								
3								
Comment								
4								
Comment								
5								
Comment								
6								
Comment								
7								
Comment								
8								
Comment								
9								
Comment								
10								
Comment								
11								
Comment								
12								
Comment								
13								
Comment								
14								
Comment								

Date	Starting Weight	Low Temp	High Temp	Food Type	Ending Weight	Rating 1=Poor 5=Great	# Caught	Game Caught
15								
Comment								

Charted Weight by Date

Weight ↓	1	2	3	4	5	6	7	8	9	10	11	12	13	14	15	
High																
Low																

Charted Performance Rating by Date

Rating ↓																
5																
4																
3																
2																
1																

Month / Year:

Date	Starting Weight	Low Temp	High Temp	Food Type	Ending Weight	Rating 1=Poor 5=Great	# Caught	Game Caught
16								
Comment								
17								
Comment								
18								
Comment								
19								
Comment								
20								
Comment								
21								
Comment								
22								
Comment								
23								
Comment								
24								
Comment								
25								
Comment								
26								
Comment								
27								
Comment								
28								
Comment								
29								
Comment								

Date	Starting Weight	Low Temp	High Temp	Food Type	Ending Weight	Rating 1=Poor 5=Great	# Caught	Game Caught
30								
Comment								
31								
Comment								

Charted Weight by Date																
Weight ↓	16	17	18	19	20	21	22	23	24	25	26	27	28	29	30	31
High																
Low																
Rating ↓	Charted Performance Rating by Date															
5																
4																
3																
2																
1																

Month / Year:

Date	Starting Weight	Low Temp	High Temp	Food Type	Ending Weight	Rating 1=Poor 5=Great	# Caught	Game Caught
1								
Comment								
2								
Comment								
3								
Comment								
4								
Comment								
5								
Comment								
6								
Comment								
7								
Comment								
8								
Comment								
9								
Comment								
10								
Comment								
11								
Comment								
12								
Comment								
13								
Comment								
14								
Comment								

Date	Starting Weight	Low Temp	High Temp	Food Type	Ending Weight	Rating 1=Poor 5=Great	# Caught	Game Caught
15								
Comment								

Charted Weight by Date

High

Weight ↓	1	2	3	4	5	6	7	8	9	10	11	12	13	14	15	
Rating ↓	Charted Performance Rating by Date															
5																
4																
3																
2																
1																

Low

Month / Year:

Date	Starting Weight	Low Temp	High Temp	Food Type	Ending Weight	Rating 1=Poor 5=Great	# Caught	Game Caught
16								
Comment								
17								
Comment								
18								
Comment								
19								
Comment								
20								
Comment								
21								
Comment								
22								
Comment								
23								
Comment								
24								
Comment								
25								
Comment								
26								
Comment								
27								
Comment								
28								
Comment								
29								
Comment								

Date	Starting Weight	Low Temp	High Temp	Food Type	Ending Weight	Rating 1=Poor 5=Great	# Caught	Game Caught
30								
Comment								
31								
Comment								

Charted Weight by Date																
Weight ↓	16	17	18	19	20	21	22	23	24	25	26	27	28	29	30	31
High																
Low																
Rating ↓	Charted Performance Rating by Date															
5																
4																
3																
2																
1																

Month / Year:

Date	Starting Weight	Low Temp	High Temp	Food Type	Ending Weight	Rating 1=Poor 5=Great	# Caught	Game Caught
1								
Comment								
2								
Comment								
3								
Comment								
4								
Comment								
5								
Comment								
6								
Comment								
7								
Comment								
8								
Comment								
9								
Comment								
10								
Comment								
11								
Comment								
12								
Comment								
13								
Comment								
14								
Comment								

Date	Starting Weight	Low Temp	High Temp	Food Type	Ending Weight	Rating 1=Poor 5=Great	# Caught	Game Caught
15								
Comment								

Charted Weight by Date																
Weight ↓	1	2	3	4	5	6	7	8	9	10	11	12	13	14	15	
High																
Low																
Rating ↓	Charted Performance Rating by Date															
5																
4																
3																
2																
1																

Month / Year:

Date	Starting Weight	Low Temp	High Temp	Food Type	Ending Weight	Rating 1=Poor 5=Great	# Caught	Game Caught
16								
Comment								
17								
Comment								
18								
Comment								
19								
Comment								
20								
Comment								
21								
Comment								
22								
Comment								
23								
Comment								
24								
Comment								
25								
Comment								
26								
Comment								
27								
Comment								
28								
Comment								
29								
Comment								

Date	Starting Weight	Low Temp	High Temp	Food Type	Ending Weight	Rating 1=Poor 5=Great	# Caught	Game Caught
30								
Comment								
31								
Comment								

Charted Weight by Date																
Weight ↓	16	17	18	19	20	21	22	23	24	25	26	27	28	29	30	31
High																
Low																
Rating ↓	Charted Performance Rating by Date															
5																
4																
3																
2																
1																

Month / Year:

Date	Starting Weight	Low Temp	High Temp	Food Type	Ending Weight	Rating 1=Poor 5=Great	# Caught	Game Caught
1								
Comment								
2								
Comment								
3								
Comment								
4								
Comment								
5								
Comment								
6								
Comment								
7								
Comment								
8								
Comment								
9								
Comment								
10								
Comment								
11								
Comment								
12								
Comment								
13								
Comment								
14								
Comment								

Date	Starting Weight	Low Temp	High Temp	Food Type	Ending Weight	Rating 1=Poor 5=Great	# Caught	Game Caught
15								
Comment								

Charted Weight by Date																
Weight ↓	1	2	3	4	5	6	7	8	9	10	11	12	13	14	15	
High																
Low																
Rating ↓	Charted Performance Rating by Date															
5																
4																
3																
2																
1																

Month / Year:

Date	Starting Weight	Low Temp	High Temp	Food Type	Ending Weight	Rating 1=Poor 5=Great	# Caught	Game Caught
16								
Comment								
17								
Comment								
18								
Comment								
19								
Comment								
20								
Comment								
21								
Comment								
22								
Comment								
23								
Comment								
24								
Comment								
25								
Comment								
26								
Comment								
27								
Comment								
28								
Comment								
29								
Comment								

Date	Starting Weight	Low Temp	High Temp	Food Type	Ending Weight	Rating 1=Poor 5=Great	# Caught	Game Caught
30								
Comment								
31								
Comment								

Charted Weight by Date																
Weight ↓	16	17	18	19	20	21	22	23	24	25	26	27	28	29	30	31
High																
Low																
Rating ↓	Charted Performance Rating by Date															
5																
4																
3																
2																
1																

Made in the USA
Middletown, DE
14 September 2021